Original title:
How I Learned to Stop Worrying and Embrace the Chaos

Copyright © 2025 Creative Arts Management OÜ
All rights reserved.

Author: Simon Fairchild
ISBN HARDBACK: 978-1-80566-075-0
ISBN PAPERBACK: 978-1-80566-370-6

Trusting the Turbulence

In a world where coffee spills,
I dance between the bills.
With socks that never match,
Chaos, an everyday catch.

I leave my keys in the fridge,
It's a life on the edge.
But in the frantic rush,
I find joy in the hush.

The Vibration of Everyday Mayhem

The cat chased the toaster,
A whirl of paws and clatter.
I waved my arms in glee,
Why worry? Just let it be!

The laundry fights back in haste,
Socks hiding, making waste.
Yet laughter fills my heart,
This mayhem's a fine art.

Shadows in the Shuffling

Life's a game of hide and seek,
With shadows that seem to peek.
A chair trips me with flair,
Yet I grin, it's all fair!

I juggle my thoughts like eggs,
Cracks and spills reveal my dregs.
So bring on the wild ride,
With laughter as my guide.

Painting the Unseen

With colors splashed on my walls,
I paint the chaos, no calls.
Splattered paint, a joyful mess,
My heart's in this crazed press!

I sip tea while it overflows,
Bubbles rise, a dance that glows.
Every drop is a delight,
In this whirlwind, I take flight.

Clarity amidst Clutter

In the midst of my socks' wild dance,
I trip over my forgotten plans.
Coffee spills, a tiny volcano,
Yet laughter blooms with every chance.

Papers flutter like confused birds,
Lost in a jungle of old receipts.
Each mess a story, absurdly heard,
Chaos sings, life skips and beats.

The Art of Unfolding

I fold my laundry with flair and pride,
Each wrinkle a secret I hide.
T-shirts tumble, a rollercoaster ride,
Life's mise-en-scène, a zany guide.

Unfolding creases, oh what fun!
My closet's a circus, every one.
A sock's missing! My race has begun,
In the chaos, I find I've won.

Chaos is a Color

Drips of paint from a clumsy brush,
Splatter artistry in a happy rush.
Murky blues meet a neon flush,
Life's wild color wheel is a must!

With mismatched socks and a chip in my cup,
I paint my day as I mix it up.
Art in the chaos, I drink from the cup,
In this vibrant mess, I'm never stuck.

Unfurling in the Unknown

I step outside in mismatched shoes,
Who needs rules when there's so much to choose?
The neighbor's dog steals my morning news,
In this wild world, I can't refuse.

I wander where the wild things roam,
With untamed thoughts that feel like home.
In the unknown, I take a comb,
Brushing through laughter, I freely roam.

Walking the Tightrope of Life

Balancing my coffee with grace,
While dodging all that life might lace.
A tumble here, a slip or two,
I laugh more than I used to do.

The high wire's thrill, oh what a view,
With squirrels as clowns, and ducks as crew.
Each wobble brings a chuckle loud,
Who knew chaos could draw a crowd?

Embracing the Beautiful Mess

Spilled paint on an artist's dream,
A splash of madness on the theme.
My socks don't match, my hair's a bird,
Yet in this tangle, joy is stirred.

Flour on my face, spaghetti in hair,
A life that's messy is beyond compare.
I dance through crumbs, a giggling spree,
This glorious chaos is wild and free.

The Joy of Serendipity

Stumbling upon a cake in the rain,
Life's little surprises break the mundane.
A wrong turn leads to ice cream galore,
Who knew that chaos could open a door?

Falling into laughter, tumbling through time,
Accidental joy, oh isn't it prime?
With every mishap, a giggle's unfurled,
Cheers to the chaos that colors my world!

Revelations from the Fractured

Shattered plates and a cat on the run,
Who knew that chaos could be such fun?
Broken mirrors reflecting delight,
In every crack, a spark shines bright.

Laughing as I gather the pieces anew,
A puzzle of giggles, with bits of blue.
With every stumble, I welcome the jest,
In the lovely chaos, I find my zest.

Trusting the Dance of Fate

Life's a waltz, a tricky spin,
Sometimes you lose, sometimes you win.
With two left feet, I trip and twirl,
Fate chuckles loud, oh what a whirl!

In mismatched socks, I dance a jig,
With each wrong step, I feel quite big.
Fate leads the way with a quirky grin,
Oh what a laugh, let the fun begin!

Finding Footing on Shifting Sand

Sand beneath, it slips away,
I leap and land, come what may.
One foot in, one foot out,
Who needs a plan when there's a shout?

The seagulls laugh, they know the score,
I dive and splat, can't help but roar.
With every slip, I gain a cheer,
Why worry too much when joy is near?

Laughter in the Midst of Chaos

While pots boil over and cats run wild,
I giggle softly, I'm chaos's child.
With cupcakes baking and flour in air,
I wear the mess like the finest wear.

Every spilled drink brings a new chance,
To dance in the puddles, a messy prance.
Chaos may rule, but so does my grin,
With laughter as my favorite din.

The Joy of Unpredictability

Plans set in ink, but rain starts to fall,
I grab my boots, I'll have a ball!
Unexpected turns make life a game,
Every twist adds a spark to the flame.

With a pie in my face and socks full of goo,
I laugh it off, it's what I do.
Embracing the weird, I find my bliss,
In life's grand dance, what's not to miss?

Embracing the Unknown

Life's a ride on roller skates,
With twists and turns at every gate.
I spill my drink and laugh aloud,
For chaos always draws a crowd.

A cat that jumps from ledge to chair,
Defying laws without a care.
I follow suit, let laughter steer,
In this wild dance, I lose my fear.

Spirals of Spontaneity

A sudden trip to unexpected places,
With mismatched socks and silly faces.
I throw caution to the breeze,
And giggle through the buzz of trees.

Dancing with a stranger's hat,
A nacho feast with crumbs like that.
Oh what fun this wildness brings,
As life reveals its secret wings.

The Calm Beneath the Clatter

In the mess, I find my zen,
A joyful chaos, time and again.
I juggle dreams and breakfast toast,
While laughing at the things that boast.

The clink of cups, the kids' loud cheer,
Music plays; I dance with fear.
In every clamor, a chance to play,
Life's a circus in its own way.

Hearts Unbound by Routine

Toss the planner, let it fly,
With whims and fancies, oh so spry.
A map of joy upon my skin,
The wacky route, that's where I begin.

I'd rather picnic on a whim,
Than count the hours, oh so grim.
So here's to life, all bright and free,
In messy love, just let it be.

Painting with Wild Strokes

My canvas bursts with colors bright,
Brush in hand, I take to flight.
A splash of red, a dash of blue,
Who knew chaos could look so true?

The paint spills over, laughter erupts,
An art show worthy of wacky hiccups.
Creativity dances, no rules to obey,
In this mad masterpiece, I paint my way.

Framed by my blunders, bold and free,
Each stroke a giggle, ridiculous glee.
If perfection's a myth, I'm a wild brush star,
Splattered in joy, just as things are.

So here's to the mess and the tangled spree,
A joyful riot, come paint with me!
Together we'll blend, mischief in tow,
In a world where calamity's the way to go.

Embracing the Untamed Journey

Once I feared the twists and turns,
But now I dance, my spirit burns.
With every bump and every sway,
I groove to life, come what may.

Maps are for those who like to know,
But I'm the wildflower in full flow.
Lost? Oh please, it's just a stroll,
Turning detours into rock and roll.

I hop on buses, miss my stops,
Chasing rainbows, dodging drops.
What's a little chaos, full of fun?
Life's a carnival, a riotous run.

So let the winds toss me about,
With giggles and shouts, I'll dance, no doubt.
For in every misstep, I find a cheer,
A thrilling ride, oh dear, oh dear!

The Liberation of Anticipation

Waking up, I check my phone,
What's today? The unknown is sewn.
My plans may blow like dandelion seed,
In chaos, I find what I truly need.

The coffee spills, my toast's a flop,
But isn't that where the fun won't stop?
I laugh out loud at the morning mess,
Anticipation's tune is pure success.

Dinner plans? A piping hot surprise,
With pizza on the ceiling, oh my, oh my!
The chaos whispers tales so grand,
Of laughter shared, hand in hand.

So here's to every wild mishap,
With giggles and grins, let's lay the map.
In this school of life, may we be the fool,
For in each wild moment, we find the jewel.

Cacophony to Clarity

Noise surrounds me—oh, what a din!
Yet in the chaos, clarity begins.
Socks mismatched, a hat on askew,
Embracing madness, it feels like new.

The world's a blur, but wait, hold tight!
Something beautiful shines in the flight.
A rooster crows, a dog's bark sings,
So loud they are, and still, joy springs.

In each laugh, and every snort,
Life's a messy, unpredictable sport.
Watch the jester spin in delight,
Turning chaos into a pinpoint of light.

So dance through the noise, skip through the clash,
For clarity blooms from the wildest bash.
With every ruckus, we celebrate here,
In the madness of life, all we need is cheer!

The Radiance of the Roughness

In a world that spins and twirls,
I tripped, I fell—oh what a whirl!
Banana peels dance on the floor,
Chaos is knocking, but I won't keep score.

Juggling tasks like a clown on a spree,
My plans all scatter like leaves from a tree.
The cat steals my lunch, what a funny heist,
In this crazy circus, I've learned to be nice.

With mischief and mayhem, I craft my delight,
Turning fumbles and flops into pure comic sight.
Each laugh a lifeboat when storms come to play,
I embrace every splash in this wild ballet.

Like a kite in the wind, I soar and I glide,
Rough edges make waves, let spontaneity ride.
So here's to the awkward, the strange, and the wild,
In the chaos, I find that I'm still just a child.

Whimsical Waves of Life

The phone rings a tune, when I'm busy to think,
A cartoonish fish gives me a wink.
Thoughts like confetti float high in the air,
I chase after dreams—who knows where they'll dare?

Ice cream erupts in a colorful mess,
Sprinkles on my shirt, I must confess.
Life's little surprises come popping like corn,
In the midst of the chaos, a new joy is born.

With socks that don't match and hair like a bird,
The beauty of chaos is perfectly absurd.
A dance on the treadmill, I spin and I sway,
In this wild ride, I won't find my way!

So join in the laughter, let worries drift by,
We'll leap like gazelles, no reason to sigh.
Each stumble's a treasure, each pratfall's a score,
In the whimsy of life, we find something more.

Surrendering to the Symphony

There once was a cat on a violin,
With paws that danced, and a whiskered grin.
Each note he plucked brought a laugh or two,
Chaos played on, as only cats do.

The dishes spun like a waltzing crew,
In the kitchen, oh what a wild brew!
Spaghetti noodles twirled like a kite,
As sauce splattered joyfully, what a sight!

A dog joined in with a woof and a bark,
They formed a band, it was a wild lark.
The rhythm of life cranked up to eleven,
In this pandemonium, I found my heaven.

With laughter and music, the world twirled round,
In the chaos of joy, my peace was found.
So I embraced the mess, let it be free,
For in the cacophony, there's glee, can't you see?

Chaotic Harmony

Meet my friend, the squirrel named Nate,
Who juggles nuts, in a twist of fate.
He drops one here, and one over there,
Yet he laughs it off—what a carefree bear!

The kids are running, making loud noise,
With sticky fingers playing with their toys.
The house may look like a battlefield,
But to their wild giggles, I must yield.

Each day's a circus, each hour a show,
With clowns and acrobats, and so much to stow.
I give up control for this wild parade,
Life's messy delight is how joy is made.

So here's to the jumbled, the silly, the loud,
To the sweet mayhem that makes me proud.
Embracing the chaos, with a wink and a grin,
In this merry madness, I let the fun in.

The Beauty of Unraveled Threads

Once I tried knitting a scarf with flair,
But tangled my yarn in a fascinating snare.
Loops and knots turned into a creature,
A funky monster—my new best feature!

The sweater I made looked more like a square,
With an armhole missing and one just bare.
Yet family wore it, so full of pride,
In my fashion disasters, they took a ride.

The buttons bounced like popcorn on the floor,
Each stitch a giggle, a joyous uproar.
I might be a mess in this knitting game,
But chaos makes art, and I'll take the fame!

So let the threads unravel, go wild and free,
For in every mishap, there's humor, you see.
Perfectly imperfect, I'm owning my style,
With laughter in stitches, it's all worth the while.

Weathering the Unknown

The weatherman said a storm would blow,
But out I ventured, with nowhere to go.
Umbrella flipped like an acrobatic feat,
As I danced in puddles, a splash-tastic treat!

Lightning flashed, and I jumped with glee,
Embracing the wildness, oh let it be.
Wind tugged at my hair, a crazy parade,
In this downpour of life, I surely won't fade.

Then raindrops sang on rooftops above,
Each patter a note of a world full of love.
With mismatched socks and a grin ear to ear,
I splashed through my fears, in rain's wild cheer.

So hail, or shine, let the elements tease,
For chaos is sunshine dressed as a breeze.
Laughing with storms, oh what a wild show,
In the dance with the crazy, my spirit will grow!

Serenity in the Storm

The wind howled like a banshee on the run,
I wore mismatched socks, thought it was fun.
Raindrops danced, splashed like little clowns,
I twirled in the puddles, forgot my frowns.

Chaos reigned with a wild, twisted glee,
The cat knocked over what used to be tea.
But in that madness, I saw lights so bright,
I laughed with the thunder, felt pure delight.

The Art of Letting Go

My planner betrayed me, it fell on the floor,
As I scrambled to catch it, it burst through the door.
The schedule was chaos, the clock said 'oh no!',
But I rolled with the punches, putting on a show.

Friends started calling, each one with a plan,
But I decided to wing it, like a happy man.
With laughter and whimsy, I glided away,
Letting go of the stress, come what may.

In the Heart of Turbulence

Turmoil was flying like socks in the night,
I dodged the disaster with all of my might.
Spilled coffee in hand, I stumbled and grinned,
Chaos was winning, but I just couldn't rescind.

The dog chased the cat, a real comedy show,
My heart did flip-flops, a real-time low blow.
Yet in that wild scene, I saw joy unfold,
A canvas of laughter, a story retold.

Finding Peace in the Pandemonium

The party erupted, balloons in the air,
I danced with abandon, without any care.
Cake flew off tables like confetti in flight,
And I laughed at the mess, what a glorious sight!

The music was blaring, laughter was shared,
In the swirl of the madness, I felt lightly bared.
With chaos embracing, I swayed to the beat,
Finding peace in the pandemonium, oh life is sweet!

Symphony of the Uncontrolled

In a world where the ducks don't line,
I chase them with snacks, oh it's divine.
The cat plays piano, steals my shoe,
And I dance like no one's watching, too.

Every note is a wobble or twist,
Life's a conductor, can't resist.
I follow the tune of a wayward breeze,
And find harmony among the bees.

Cacophony reigns, it's perfectly clear,
As I laugh at the chaos, fizzle, and cheer.
Orchestrating the madness is pure delight,
In a playground of blunders, I take flight.

So join the parade, let's stumble and sway,
Embrace the absurd in the silliest way.
Grab a donut, a broom, let's prance around,
In this symphony lost, life's joy can be found.

Chaos: My Co-pilot

In my trusty car, chaos takes the wheel,
Riding shotgun with a zest that's unreal.
GPS? Nah, it's a wild, winding road,
With every wrong turn, new stories unfold.

The map's just a suggestion, a wild kind of joke,
As I navigate life like a woeful bloke.
Spilled coffee's the splash paint on my soul,
Making art of the mess—what a glorious goal!

My co-pilot laughs, gives me a wink,
As we swerve through the troubles, we hardly think.
With every detour, more joy's on display,
In this whirlwind of life, let the chaos play.

So here's to the bumpy, unpredictable ride,
To the laughter and joy, let's cast worry aside.
With chaos beside me, I'm ready to roll,
In this comedic ballet, I find my control.

Ebb and Flow of Fate

The tides of my plans come in and out,
Like socks in the dryer, there's often a doubt.
I build castles of sand, only to watch,
As the waves bring them down—oh, what a botch!

A dance with the tide, a humorous waltz,
Life's foamy embrace never finds a fault.
I surf on the chaos, it's quite the ride,
With laughter and craziness as my guide.

Fortune's a joker, playing tricks on me,
A twist of fate, and oh, what glee!
Roll with the punches, I take a deep breath,
In the ebb of the chaos, I find life and death.

So bring on the waves, let's crash and collide,
In this ocean of madness, I shall abide.
With a grin on my face, I welcome the fate,
In the ebb and flow, I find room to create.

The Sweetness of Surrender

I tossed my plans into the breeze,
Watched them flutter like butterflies, with ease.
The universe chuckled, then slapped me with glee,
As I clutched my popcorn, a movie to see.

My hair's a tornado, my shirt's inside out,
Yet here I am, laughing, while others pout.
I roll with the punches, drop the façade,
Surrendering joyously to what's oddly flawed.

Flip-flops mismatched, but it matters not,
In the chaos I dance, every tumble I've got.
Life's candy-coated bliss wrapped in a mess,
In the sweetness of surrender, I find my success.

So join me in laughter, let go of the reins,
In this carnival ride, we'll embrace all the pains.
Worry? Never! Let's twirl with the breeze,
In the sweetness of surrender, we'll do as we please.

Breathing through the Noise

In the frenzy of the day, I grin,
Chaos dances, where do I begin?
Juggling tasks like a circus clown,
I'll wear these worries, like a funky crown.

With a twirl and a leap, I lose control,
Checklists crumpled in a coffee bowl.
Embrace the wildness, let laughter flow,
For in the mess, true joy starts to grow.

Unscripted Journeys

Maps are forged in the winds of fate,
Sometimes I stumble, but I'm never late.
Each unexpected turn brings a laugh,
Twists and turns make for a perfect path.

U-turns and wrong ways, a thrilling spree,
Life's improv show, come laugh with me!
Who needs a script for this crazy ride?
With a wink and a grin, I take it in stride.

The Stillness in the Surge

Riding the waves of a raucous sea,
Finding calm in the chaos, just let it be.
Like a surfer on a wild, foamy crest,
I find my peace, it's all for the best.

Between the rush and the hush, I sway,
Dodging the worries that come my way.
In the whirlpool of life, I'll do my dance,
With every spin, I give joy a chance.

Painting with Uncertainty

With a brush dipped in spontaneity,
I splash the canvas, living frantically.
Each stroke a giggle, a wobble, a sway,
Colors collide in a bright ballet.

Who needs perfection in this artful spree?
Muddled hues tell tales, wild and free.
In the mess of creation, I find delight,
For chaos blooms flowers that feel so right.

Celebrating the Unraveled

Life's a sock with missing pairs,
A puzzle with no end, who cares?
Dance in circles, chase your tail,
Join the circus, love the fail.

Tomorrow's secrets, feel so bold,
Life's a mess, or so I'm told.
Paint your worries bright and loud,
Spin the chaos, join the crowd.

Thoughts are clouds that drift and play,
They change their shape, then float away.
Embrace the lunacy in sight,
Each stumble leads to laughter's light.

So raise a glass to joyful strife,
Here's to the fun in our mad life!
With every twist, a giggle sparks,
Let's dance in parks till after dark.

Breathe into the Whirl

Worries whirl like leaves in wind,
I catch them all, or so I pretend.
A juggler's act, my life's a show,
With pies and clowns, oh what a glow!

Spin, twirl, and take a leap,
Jump into chaos, it's ours to keep.
With every laugh, the clouds will part,
Feel the rhythm; trust your heart.

Stumble, tumble, fall, then rise,
With every mishap, a sweet surprise.
The world's a stage, absurd, and grand,
Join the dance; together we stand.

Sometimes I grin, sometimes I frown,
But always in my clownish gown.
Cackles echo, fears retreat,
In charming chaos, life's a treat!

Portrait of the Chaotic Soul

My mind's a canvas, splashed and bold,
Painted worries, stories told.
A funny hat, mismatched shoes,
Chaos reigns, yet who'd refuse?

Life's a recipe, mix it right,
Add a dash of sheer delight.
Whisk your fears into the stew,
Laughter's seasoning, a perfect brew.

Splash! There goes another plan,
But I'm okay; I'm still the man.
With every hiccup, joy will bloom,
In pandemonium, I find my room.

So paint your mixture, swirl it 'round,
Find your magic in the sound.
Embrace the mess, don't take the toll,
Raise your brush—be chaotic soul!

Acceptance beneath the Surface

Under the waves, where chaos sways,
I found acceptance in wild displays.
With each bubble, a worry flies,
In the deep, where laughter lies.

Boat oars splashing, a comical scene,
Navigating tides, I sail between.
With every wobble and wild ride,
I learn to laugh and not to hide.

Embrace the whirlpool, dance with the tide,
With fishy friends, I will reside.
Under the surface, joy's the theme,
Wrestling chaos, living the dream.

So here's to ripples, here's to waves,
To joyful chaos that life engraves.
In every splash, there's fun to find,
Acceptance swims in the chaotic mind.

Glories of the Unplanned

A soup of socks upon the floor,
Dinner plans? They're just folklore.
The cat's in charge, it seems to me,
As I trip on shoes, oh what glee!

Surprises jump from every nook,
Who knew my life was such a book?
With coffee spilled and shoes untied,
I laugh aloud, I'll take the ride.

My plans escape like bubbles blown,
Adventures wait in chaos grown.
A dance with fate, a silly waltz,
Life's wild, and that's our fault!

So let them rain, the whims of fate,
Unplanned days? They're truly great.
With joy in chaos, I find my spin,
In glorious mess, my life begins!

Seeds in the Storm

Raindrops tapped upon my head,
A dance of chaos, no words to dread.
Puddles form like cheerful pools,
I leap right in; who needs the rules?

Wind-chimes sing in offbeat tunes,
My umbrella's upside-down—what a boon!
Socks mismatched, but spirits high,
In storms I find my reason why.

The garden grows with weeds galore,
But flowers pop; who could ask for more?
A little mess can bring such cheer,
Seeds of laughter sprout year by year.

Chaos seeds, they twirl and spin,
In wildest winds, the fun begins.
So here's to storms, bring on the squall,
In nature's chaos, we'll have a ball!

Melodies of the Unconventional

Off-beat rhythm, life's a tune,
Dancing squirrels beneath the moon.
No sheet music for this song,
But every note feels right, not wrong.

In mismatched shoes, I tap my feet,
Marching through life with quirky beat.
Hear the laugh of a bubbling brook,
It sings to me, oh what a hook!

Random notes fly through the air,
A joker's jester without a care.
Life's concert hall is never bland,
With chaos as the house band.

So grab your friends, let's play along,
In the melody, we all belong.
The tune of life might twist and bend,
But in this chaos, we transcend!

Fragments in Full Bloom

My plan was neat, a lovely stack,
But then the dog took it all back.
Scraps of paper scattered wide,
Yet in this mess, my dreams reside.

A quilt of colors, patchy, bright,
Each patch a story, a silly plight.
With popcorn ceiling and stickers on walls,
I find that joy in chaos calls.

Fractured pieces take the shape,
Of laughter spilling from escape.
Embracing all that life might throw,
In tangled threads, true bliss does grow.

So here's to chaos, wild and free,
In every fragment, there's harmony.
With mismatched socks and crooked lines,
I bloom in chaos, and that's just fine!

The Freedom of Fluctuation

Woke up today, socks don't match,
Coffee spilled, oh what a catch!
Pants lost in the dryer spree,
I guess I'll wear my pink ones, whee!

Plans went south, a sudden rain,
Neighbors dancing in the lane.
Life's a circus, come join the show,
With popcorn and laughter, let's go with the flow!

Who knew chaos could be so sweet?
Like an unexpected birthday treat.
Twists and turns, I laugh along,
In this wild ride, I'm never wrong!

So here I stand, arms open wide,
Embracing storms, with nothing to hide.
Freedom found in the loopy race,
Let the world spin, I've found my place!

Embracing the Unpredictable

Alarm clock's broken, what a flair,
Looming deadlines, I just don't care!
Breakfast was cereal, chocolate bliss,
Spilled some milk, a gorgeous miss!

Traffic jams, I sing aloud,
To my own tune, feeling proud.
Puddle jumping, oh what fun,
Dancing 'neath the cloudy sun!

Unexpected guests, pizza delight,
Board games erupt into playful fights.
Who knew life could be so grand?
With twists and giggles, unplanned!

So let the tides rise and fall,
Embrace the chaos, answer the call.
For in the madness, joy is near,
Dance along, my dear, my dear!

Unchained from the Routine

Alarm? Nah, I'll skip that sound,
Socks on my hands? Sculpting profound!
Breakfast? Or just a donut spree,
Life's much better in a fantasy!

Spontaneity's my funky dance,
Forward, backward, taking a chance.
Who needs a map when you've got flair?
Let's lose the route, embrace the air!

Tangled hair, mismatched shoes,
Every day's a brand-new muse.
Chasing whims, just fooling around,
An unchained heart, unbound, unbound!

So here's to ruckus, laughter, and fun,
In the rollercoaster we've just begun.
Forget the rules and join the spree,
Life's a spice, come taste with me!

A Dance Among the Shadows

Tiptoe through the quirky night,
Stars above, oh what a sight!
Moonlight twinkles, casting charms,
While chaos hugs with open arms.

Whimsical whispers, shadows play,
Dancing dreams that lead the way.
Life's a jest, a vibrant ballet,
Who knew the mess could save the day?

Clumsy pirouettes, laughter rolls,
Stumbling along, embracing our roles.
With every twist, a story unfolds,
In the chaos, pure gold beholds!

So let's celebrate the wild unknown,
In this dance, we've beautifully grown.
Every misstep, a joyous cheer,
In the shadows, we're all pioneers!

Unraveled Yet Whole

Life's a puzzle, pieces fly,
Missing parts, oh me, oh my!
But in the chaos, I find my way,
Laughter blooms, come what may.

Socks in the dryer, a rogue sock thief,
I find my joy, a moment of relief.
A tangle of strings, a game in disguise,
Who knew life's mess could bring such surprise?

Juggling tasks, like tossing a pie,
Sometimes it's messy, and that's just fine!
Lemonade spills, dance in the glare,
For every worry, there's something to share.

So here's to chaos, a wild, sweet ride,
With laughter and fun, I'll take it in stride.
Unraveled, yet whole, with each little twist,
Life's whimsical dance is too good to miss!

Moments of Serene Turbulence

A squirrel on a skateboard, zooming past,
Life's little surprises, they come so fast.
Mismatched shoes, a style all my own,
In this messy garden, my laughter has grown.

Spilled coffee on my shirt, a brand new design,
Chaos fuels giggles, oh isn't it fine?
Twisting and turning, a circus I know,
Stumbling through moments, a comedic show.

To-do lists like origami, folded just right,
But who needs structure? Let's dance through the night!
Rain on my window, a rhythm so sweet,
In the storm I find solace, a song on repeat.

Chaos, my friend, with your colorful hues,
You teach me to smile, even when I lose.
So bring on the frenzy, let's take it in stride,
In each whirlwind moment, true joy will reside!

Embracing the Whirlwind

A cat in a box, it's quite a fine sight,
Finding joy in the wildest of nights.
Mistaken directions, oh what a thrill,
In every detour, I find a new skill.

Weather alerts, a storm's coming near,
But I'll twirl and dance without a single fear.
My hair's a tornado, a style by chance,
In this playful chaos, I'll take a wild dance.

Laundry as mountains, socks looking lost,
In the comedy of life, I'm happy at all cost.
Jumping through puddles, embrace every splash,
In the chaos of life, let's make it a bash!

With giggles and wiggles in every odd twist,
The best kind of fun is hiding in mist.
So here's to the whirlwind, bring on your game,
In laughter and chaos, I'll dance just the same!

Dancing with Disorder

Pancakes flipped high, one sticks to the wall,
Breakfast ballet, I'm ready for it all!
With spoon in my pocket and flour on my nose,
I embrace the mayhem, it's how the fun grows.

A mismatched puzzle, colors so bright,
Filling in gaps, hey, that'll feel right!
Life's a circus, I'm front row for fun,
With clowns and confetti, the show has begun.

Rain boots in summer, I'll splash if I dare,
In the chaos of laughter, there's magic to share.
Time slips away like ice cream on toast,
In moments like these, I'm grateful the most.

So here's to the clatter, to tripping and stumbles,
To dancing through chaos, where joy never crumbles.
With each joyful mess, the heart starts to sing,
Embracing disorder, oh, what joy it can bring!

Dancing in the Storm

Raindrops tap on my head, oh what a show,
I twirl like a tornado, just letting it go.
Umbrellas upside down, a hat became drenched,
Laughing at thunder, my worries all clenched.

Lightning's a disco, the sky's a big stage,
I put on my socks with a matching green page.
My dance steps are shuffled, all rhythm is lost,
But what is a storm if not fun at the cost?

Puddles like mirrors, reflecting my glee,
Splashes turned laughter, I'm wild and I'm free.
Forget about timing, that's all tossed away,
I'm the storm's best friend; let's dance here today!

So when the clouds rumble and the winds start to play,
I'll join in the ruckus, let the wildness sway.
With chaos as music, I'll bounce and I'll twirl,
In this wet, wild world, watch my laughter unfurl.

Serendipity's Embrace

I woke up this morning, socks mismatched twice,
Tripped over breakfast, oh that's not so nice.
Coffee's too strong, like a punch to the face,
But chuckles abound in this bustling race.

Tangled up schedules, my plans are a mess,
But that's where the fun lies, I must confess.
A stumble through life, with giggles and sighs,
Each twist in my path holds a sweet surprise.

Spilled paint on my shirt, now I'm a new trend,
Artistic? I'd say so, it's lovely, my friend.
Lost keys in the fridge? That's a neat little trick,
Laughing my way through the day's little hic.

So come on, dear chaos, let's dance through the fray,
With serendipity leading, we'll sway and we'll play.
Life's greatest adventure is found in the bends,
In clumsy encounters, we find our best friends.

The Beauty of Uncertainty

In the fog of the morning, I'm lost as can be,
But hold on, what's this? A squirrel laughs at me.
With jumbles of "oops" and some twisted luck,
I'm rolling through life like a hapless old truck.

Plans on a napkin, scribbles and doodles,
But waves of confusion? Oh, what's life without noodles?

Slip on a banana, oh what a scene,
Uncertainty's spark makes my soul feel so keen.

Each turn's like a game show, spin that big wheel,
I'd say "what's my prize?" But there's no need to feel.
Laughter erupts as the plot thickens fast,
With chaos as partner, I'm free and I'm vast.

So here's to the unknown, the wild and the bright,
Where chaos is palatable, day dances with night.
I'll wear my confusion like a crown of pure fun,
For the beauty of life lies in all that's undone.

Chaos as my Compass

Lost in the maze of toys on my floor,
I plot out my journey with giggles and snore.
The map's a little messy, okay, quite a lot,
But who needs directions? I'm loving the plot.

Like pirate ships sailing on seas made of fudge,
With jellybeans guiding where I won't budge.
A treasure map scribbled in colors so bright,
With chaos as compass, I'll steer through the night.

The path may be wobbly, it twists like a joke,
But laughter's my anchor; chaos is broke.
Every stumble's a dance, every misstep's a cheer,
In the grand scheme of chaos, I'm the captain here!

So here's to the chaos, the wild, and the free,
With giggles aplenty, oh, what fun it will be!
I'll chart my own course through each twist and bend,
For with chaos as guide, I see no end.

In the Embrace of Turmoil

Life's a circus, I'm the clown,
Juggling worries, upside down.
My pie in the sky turned to fluff,
Yet here I dance, that's just enough.

Socks that don't match? Who even cares?
I wear them proudly, end all stares.
Each bump and trip, a giggle spree,
In chaos, I find my glee and glee.

Caffeine spills and cracked old screens,
Chaos reigns in my daydreams.
But laughter bubbles through the mess,
I raise my cup, I must confess.

So bring the storms, let lightning strike,
I'll be the star of the mic.
In turmoil's arms, I claim my throne,
A jester's heart but never alone.

Lighthouse in the Fog

Waves are crashing, boats are swayed,
But in the fog, my fears parade.
With snacks in hand and tunes on blast,
I navigate through chaos fast.

The lighthouse beeps, a charming tune,
Guiding me under the silly moon.
I dance on deck with ice cream in tow,
What'll happen next? Who the heck knows!

Seagulls cackle, in a feathery fight,
While I sip coffee with sheer delight.
Misting laughter through salty air,
Each chaotic moment is beyond compare.

So here I stand, rain-soaked and free,
Sailing chaos like a bumblebee.
With fog horns blaring in my ears,
I giggle, I twirl, void all fears.

Tides of Temptation

Oh, the tides may rise and fall,
I'll surf those waves, I'll heed the call.
With ice cream cones and tangled hair,
In temptations' grip, I lounge with flair.

Chocolate drips on my sunny dress,
Who knew chaos could be such a mess?
I chase the waves with silly fun,
Grinning wide, like I've already won.

Sea stars laugh, they twinkle bright,
While I try to catch them; what a sight!
Each splash and swerve, my heart will race,
In turmoil I find my happy place.

So ride the currents, let it flow,
I'm on this boat, and I'm ready to go.
In tides of folly, sweet escapade,
With laughter as a cozy barricade.

Whispers of the Wild Wind

Wind is howling, trees do sway,
But I just grin, it's my kind of play.
With hair like a bird's nest, wild and free,
In chaos I find my remedy.

Baking chaos like a frenzied chef,
Mixing flour while I laugh so deaf.
I stumble, bumble, and giggle bright,
Each mix-up just adds to my delight.

Chasing clouds that dance in the air,
While giggles escape without a care.
With nature's breath tickling my cheek,
In this wildness, I've found the peak.

So let the wind pull me along,
In each sway, I find my song.
Embracing chaos, silly and bold,
In whispers of wind, my heart turns gold.

Wading through the Wild Waters

In a boat with no paddle, I drift along,
The river's a rollercoaster, wild and wrong.
Fish jump like they know my fears,
While I'm giggling and shedding tears.

The sharks wear tiny party hats,
As I sing to the dancing spats.
Waves crash while I splash and shout,
This chaotic ride, oh what it's about!

Rafts pop like balloons in the sun,
But hey, I've made a splash and had my fun.
With ice cream dreams and jelly fish,
In muddy waters, I feel quite swish.

Through whirlpools and eddies, I glide with glee,
Navigating life, like a fish in tea.
So here's to the chaos, my faith on display,
I'll ride this wild water, come what may!

Heartbeats in the Unknown

Under the stars, I stroll alone,
Every shadow feels like a drone.
Yet I embrace each anxious chase,
For laughter bursts in this curious space.

Monsters in the closet throw me a grin,
As I dip my toes, let the fun begin.
With every heartbeat, I dance and sway,
In the chaos of night, I find my play.

A leap into laughter, a slide into joy,
I'm no longer the cautious, uptight little boy.
Shaking off jitters, I take to the floor,
In this unpredictable game, I always want more.

The unknown is silly, with giggles abound,
I stumble and tumble, and fall to the ground.
Yet through all the chaos, I manage to groan,
Cheers to the wild, for I'm never alone!

The Magic in the Messiness

Paint splatters on my favorite chair,
A masterpiece made with moments rare.
Through spills and thrills, I laugh till I cry,
In this messy world, I learn how to fly.

Cookies burnt and floors adorned with dough,
Kitchen disasters are my buoyant show.
I holler with joy as the cake shakes its crumbs,
Chaos and laughter, a waltz that hums.

Sticky fingers and cheeky grins,
Life's sweetest moments come from the sins.
With icing fights and flour clouds,
I make merry with my chaotic crowds.

So here's to the spills, the globs, the spry,
In each little mess, I find my high.
For in the maelstrom, magic resides,
Here's to the process, where chaos abides!

Fireflies in the Friction

On a road full of bumps, I ride my bike,
With every jolt, I feel more alike.
Fireflies burst in neon delight,
Painting the darkness, oh what a sight!

The tires squeak and bounce on the ground,
In chaos I find the joy that I've found.
Riding through laughter, I dare to be bold,
With each little wobble, my spirit won't fold.

Swerving through nonsense with flair and grace,
Wearing chaos like it's my best lace.
So I giggle and wiggle, letting it flow,
With fireflies lighting up all that I know.

Embracing the bumps as part of the ride,
In the chaos and friction, I take in my stride.
So here's to the sparks and wild little heights,
In the dance of the chaos, I find my delights!

The Wisdom of Uncertainty

Life's a game, you can't control,
When plans go south, just roll with the whole.
Tossing coins and flipping words,
Who knew chaos comes with birds?

Embrace the mess, it's quite a show,
Dancing through the ebb and flow.
With every twist, there's laughter's spark,
A wild ride from dawn till dark.

Count your ducks that won't align,
In their quack, you'll find the fine.
Worry less, be free, take flight,
In the whirlwind, laugh with delight.

So here's the key, it isn't hard,
Life's a circus, you're the bard.
Trust the chaos, find the cheer,
With every tumble, joy draws near.

Unfolding the Frayed Edges

My plans unraveled like old yarn,
A tapestry of slight disarm.
With every thread, a funny twist,
In luck's great game, I can't resist.

Chasing dreams on runaway trains,
Bumping along through silly lanes.
Stitching up a patchwork quilt,
With every rip, a laugh is built.

Life's a puzzle with missing parts,
But scrappy solutions fill our hearts.
With frayed edges, a charming view,
Who knew chaos could feel so new?

So take a sip from your wild cup,
Let fears fade as you lift up.
In the fray, joy's the prize,
Embrace the giggles, don't despise.

Finding Tranquility in Tumult

In storms of noise and busy streets,
I find my calm in dancing beats.
With honks and shouts as my backdrop,
I spin and twirl, I never stop.

Chaos swirls like leaves in fall,
I laugh and leap, I heed the call.
Balance found in wobbly air,
With giddy leaps, I float with flair.

When things go wrong, I throw confetti,
In life's mad race, I feel quite ready.
With every hiccup, I take a bow,
The stage belongs to chaos now.

So sip your drink, and ride the flow,
In chaos, there's an art to show.
With giggles bouncing, hearts set free,
In the tumult, find your glee.

Riding the Waves of Mayhem

Life's a surf on shifting tides,
With every wave, a laugh abides.
Catch a foam of jokes afloat,
In the chaos, I find my boat.

So grab your board, let's take the plunge,
Through crazy curls, we'll laugh and lunge.
Smiles replace the need for frown,
In this wild ride, we won't drown.

Banana peels and jokes collide,
With each wipeout, take in the ride.
With grit and grace, we'll find our way,
In the mayhem, we will play.

So raise your hands to the sky,
Ride the waves, just let them fly.
In chaos, there's a curious charm,
Buckle up, we're safe from harm.

Harmony in the Haphazard

In the kitchen, flour flies,
I try to cook, but can only cry.
Pasta sticks to the ceiling,
Dinner's now a farce, revealing.

My socks don't match, a wondrous sight,
Each morning's a colorful fight.
I laugh at these mismatched shoes,
Maybe chaos is good news.

Cats chase shadows, dogs bark loud,
A ruckus spirals, drawing a crowd.
In this joyful mess, I see my prize,
Life's not perfect, but oh, what a rise!

So I'll dance in the chaos, twirl with glee,
Every bump is a chance to be free.
With giggles and grins, I take my stance,
In uncertainty, I'll always dance.

Glimpses of Grace in the Hectic

The alarm never rings, but I'm awake,
My coffee spills, oh for heaven's sake!
I trip on the cat, he gives me a glare,
In this wild circus, life's a dare.

A haircut gone wrong, I laugh with the crew,
"My name's not Einstein, I 'do' what I do!"
With scissors and tape, I risk the unknown,
Each style a statement, I'm never alone.

Traffic jams turn into karaoke nights,
The car becomes a stage, as the sun ignites.
With honks as the bass and the road signs as cue,
We'll sing to the heavens, just me and my crew.

In moments of chaos, glimpses of grace,
Turns out that trouble's a charming embrace.
I'll tiptoe and tumble, with laughter as sound,
In this circus of life, joy's always around.

The Dance of Disarray

Under the disco ball of the living room,
I chaotically clean, while the dust bunnies bloom.
A sock on the ceiling, a shoe in the fridge,
I twirl past the clutter like it's an old ridge.

Dinner plans flop into pure comedy,
Spaghetti turns to soup, oh what a melody!
With noodles dancing off plates like a spree,
I savor the chaos, like fine elderberry.

Laundry's a puzzle, what goes where?
I'm lost in the fabric, with colors that flare.
Whites now sport pinks, like carnival dreams,
In this shuffle of garments, life bursts at the seams.

So join in the chaos, let yourself sway,
There's laughter in the mess, don't shy away.
With each twist and turn, I take a stance,
In the dance of disarray, I find my chance.

Finding Gold in the Grit

Life's got grit, like sand in my shoe,
But I sift through the chaos, find treasures anew.
A lost coffee mug, now an art piece bold,
In this gritty life, stories unfold.

Falling with style, like a comedy show,
I brush off the dirt—what a way to go!
I slip and I slide, what a grand old time,
In these little mishaps, I'm living my rhyme.

Juggling work calls with a pizza surprise,
My desk's a mad circus, oh how time flies!
In this joyful tumble, I learn to embrace,
The splashes of chaos, life's vibrant grace.

With every mishap, I gather some gold,
Rich in the laughter, and stories retold.
So here's to the grit, the fumbles, the flaws,
In the fabric of life, I find my applause.

Wait for the Daybreak

Every morning, I trip on my shoelace,
A dance with disaster, a sprinting race.
Coffee spills, I laugh at the mess,
Who knew a morning could be such a test?

Clouds above are plotting my day,
They giggle softly, 'Oh, look at him play.'
But I'm a jester in this chaos spree,
Feeling giggly, I let my heart be free.

The sun peeks in, a cheeky grin,
Chasing shadows away with a spin.
My worries vanish, like birds in flight,
Maybe chaos knows how to make things right.

So when night falls, and chaos ignites,
I'll dance with my fears, with all of their bites.
Tomorrow's a promise, a chance to be brave,
Embracing the silly, the wild, and the rave.

Making Peace with the Unruly

A sock goes missing, it's a mystery plain,
The other's laughing, it's gone with the rain.
Socks in rebellion, refusing to pair,
I turn on my playlist, who needs to care?

The cat's in the cupboard, the dog's on the floor,
Chaos is knocking at every door.
Life's a sitcom, I'm the clown in the frame,
I roll off the couch and I'm never the same.

Plants on the counter, they've taken a stand,
Growing in chaos, as nature had planned.
I'm but a guest in this wild, crazy show,
With laughter as currency, I'll help it all grow.

With each little mishap, I take it in stride,
The unruly chaos is my joyful guide.
Messy and loud, I embrace the array,
I'll dance through the riot, come what may.

Sails Unfurled in the Tempest

Windy and wild, my boat takes a spin,
With sails like a dancer, I'm plunged right in.
The sea laughs loudly, the waves have a roar,
I hold on tight, who knows what's in store?

Fish jump around, like they're out for a game,
While I'm the captain, but I'm not really tame.
Crashing and splashing, I'm feeling alive,
With chaos swirling, I learn how to thrive.

The clouds gather 'round, they're plotting a show,
Lightning's the spotlight, it's all part of the flow.
Each splash of water, a note in the song,
The tempest takes charge, but it can't be wrong.

So here I am, sailing storms in glee,
With chaos my compass, I feel wild and free.
When the day's done, and the waves settle low,
I'll chuckle and toast to the storm's crazy glow.

The Gentle Embrace of Disarray

Pancakes flipping, and the syrup's a splash,
The kitchen's a circus, but I'm having a bash.
Eggs in a scramble, the whisk is a blur,
Every moment chaotic, a smile's a stir.

A puzzle's missing pieces, oh what a game,
The cat's found a corner and thinks it's the same.
I throw my hands up in a melodramatic way,
Life's not a lineup; there's joy in the fray.

My laundry's a rainbow, a dance on the floor,
Each color tells stories of chaos galore.
Instead of frustration, I giggle and sigh,
For laughter's the answer to every 'Oh my!'

So here's to the moments all tangled and bright,
The gentle embrace of sweet, silly light.
With a wink in my heart and a skip in my day,
I'll gallivant boldly, come what may!

Finding Peace in the Whirlwind

In the midst of a storm, I found my dance,
Spinning on tables, who needs a plan?
Coffee spilling, laughter in the air,
Oh look, there goes my lunch—beware!

Flip-flops flying, chaos leading the way,
I might lose my keys, but hey, it's okay!
Raincoat is missing, oh what a sight,
I'll glide through the puddles, feeling just right!

Socks unmatched and hair in a frizz,
I smile at the mess, it's just how it is.
A dance in the kitchen, I twirl with glee,
Who needs perfection? Just let it be!

With every mishap, a chuckle I find,
The whirlwind of life is uniquely designed.
So let's toast to chaos, let joy take the wheel,
In the whirlwind of life, I'm learning to feel!

Letting Go of the Tides

Sailed on a boat with a hopeful grin,
But the winds took a turn, lost my place again!
Flip-flopped my way through the ocean's embrace,
Caught in the tides, yet I still found my space.

Seagulls are screeching, my snack's in their beaks,
It's a comedy show, with laughs and some squeaks.
A wave for my worries, a splash for my fears,
I'm surfing through chaos, with giggles and cheers!

Nothing is certain, oh what a ride!
My sunscreen's misplaced, and my boat's on the side.
But with every flip, I just ride with the tides,
A captain of chaos, where laughter resides!

So here's to our journeys, wild as they seem,
I'll anchor my ship on a light-hearted dream.
Letting go of the tides, with a wink and a jig,
In the dance of the waves, life's never too big!

Revelations in Disorder

Messy hair, don't care, what a carefree style,
Juggling the chaos, I've learned with a smile.
A sock on my hand, a hat on my cat,
Oh, this life is a circus, and I'm loving that!

Epic fails in the kitchen, a soufflé to the floor,
Pasta's a noodle fight, oh let's start a war!
I'll whip up the laughter, sprinkle it bright,
When chaos is cooking, it feels so right!

Plans like confetti, they scatter and fly,
Embracing the chaos, I reach for the sky.
Dance in my slippers while the dishes await,
In the mess, I discover my own special fate!

So here's to the madness, the laughter, the fun,
In the art of disorder, I'm second to none.
With joy in the chaos, my heart starts to sing,
Revelations of life, like a wild, joyous fling!

The Art of Surrender

When plans take a nose-dive, oh what a show,
I find that it's better to just go with the flow.
Spilled milk and giggles, my motto—be brave,
In the land of surrender, I happily wave.

Picture me juggling, the world's out of line,
With a pie on my face, I say, "It's divine!"
The universe laughs, as I trip on my feet,
In the chaos of life, I find my own beat!

Maps are for amateurs, I wander and glide,
With a heart full of mischief, I laugh and I stride.
So let's toast to the blunders, the madcap delight,
In the art of surrender, everything feels right!

Covered in frosting, a cake that got flipped,
With a grin on my face, let no moment be skipped.
In this circus of living, I'm joyful, not shy,
The art of surrender, oh my, oh my!

The Unexpected Canvas

Life's a canvas, splashed with paint,
Colors blend, and nothing's quaint.
Streaks of chaos, wild and free,
A masterpiece of irony.

In spilled coffee, I find delight,
As my cat joins the morning fight.
Doodles dance across the floor,
Who needs plans when there's so much more?

Laughter echoes, the fridge falls closed,
With every blunder, joy exposed.
Mix-up all the shades and hues,
Let's toast to the beauty of the blues!

So grab your brush, don't play it safe,
Life's a riot, join the waif.
From every stumble, I take my cue,
Chaos paints, and I play too!

Reveling in the Ruckus

Amidst the ruckus, I find my groove,
Twists and turns, oh how they move!
Juggling socks and scattered dreams,
Oh, life, you're bursting at the seams!

Each wrong turn feels like a dance,
Led by whimsy, oh what a chance!
I laugh at plans that go awry,
What's a little chaos? Just a pie in the sky!

Cadence of chaos, my heartbeats race,
Embrace the blunders in their place.
Life's a circus with no tightrope,
I swing from laughter to boundless hope!

So here's to muddles, can't keep them down,
With a silly grin, I wear the crown.
Let all the mayhem come my way,
I'll party with chaos, come what may!

Mastering the Meltdown

In the kitchen, my soufflé's a flop,
Eggs and flour go splat with a pop.
Pans collide in a clanking show,
I'll laugh at the mess, let the chaos flow!

Meltdown moments bring giggles with ease,
Like a blender fight that spills my peas.
Every kitchen nightmare, a tale to share,
As I dance 'round the mess, without a care!

With pots as drums, I conjure a beat,
Baking blunders don't taste so sweet.
But oh, the laughter that fills the walls,
Who needs perfection? It's chaos that calls!

So let the eggs crack and the batter fly,
Life in the kitchen's an open sky.
From every meltdown, take a big bite,
In this wobbly dance, oh what a sight!

Chaos as a Teacher

In chaos's embrace, I've found my way,
Lessons learned, come what may.
Life's a puzzle, mismatched pieces,
From every chaos, confidence increases.

With muddy shoes and a crooked smile,
I stumble forward, mile after mile.
Plans are whimsical as clouds that drift,
Yet in the wild, I find my gift!

So here's to life, messy and bright,
Each blunder adds a new delight.
With every hiccup and silly spree,
Chaos, my teacher, sets me free!

I raise my glass to each wild day,
Here's to the bumps that guide my way.
In every swirl and twirl, I see,
A world of laughter that welcomes me!

Breathe

In the midst of a storm, I found a sigh,
Like a balloon in the sky, I dared to fly.
Laughter erupted from chaos so wild,
    Even my worries felt like a child.

Bubbles of joy danced, unbound and free,
Tickling my senses, oh, can't you see?
Scribbling my fears on a napkin tonight,
And tossing them out with all of my might.

Frogs in my throat croaked songs of delight,
While juggling my worries in evening light.
With a wink and a grin, I marched into the fray,
    Who knew chaos could be such a play?

Each breath a whisper, a giggle, a shout,
Learning to wander, let silly doubts out.
The more I embrace it, the lighter I feel,
    In this wacky circus, oh, life is a meal!

Believe

Like marshmallows in soup, dreams float on high,
With sprinkles of magic and a wink of the eye.
Each stumble is laughter, a whimsical chance,
Who knew that chaos could lead to a dance?

Floating on whimsy, I twirl with a grin,
With rubber duck friends, the chaos begins.
Imagination's a rollercoaster ride,
So hold on tight, let the giggles decide.

Believing in nonsense, I'm free as a kite,
With socks that don't match, oh what a sight!
I'll dive into puddles, let rain have its say,
For joy blooms in mayhem, come join the fray!

In the jungle of laughter, I roar with delight,
Trusting the chaos banishes fright.
So let all those worries drift far away,
For life is a playground, come out and play!

Become

In a world full of whimsy, I take a chance,
To become an acrobat in a silly dance.
With socks on my ears and a hat on my cat,
I find joy in chaos—it's where I'm at!

Unicorns prance through this curious haze,
While jellybeans scatter in ridiculous ways.
I'll put on a crown made of spaghetti and cheese,
And wear craziness proudly, if it can please.

Awkward and lost, a beautiful mess,
In the realm of the wild, I find happiness.
Becoming a dreamer with glittery flair,
I'll summon the chaos and dance in midair.

So just close your eyes, and dive in headfirst,
For the splashes of life are a whimsical burst.
In this carnival vibe, we laugh and we roam,
Embracing the madness, we're never alone!

Whispers of Wildness

The whispers of wildness, they call out to me,
In rustling leaves, there's a giggling spree.
With squirrels as my buddies, I'm ready to leap,
Dancing through chaos where secrets can creep.

Armadillos in tutus twirl under the moon,
And I join their party, I'm over the moon!
With chaos as my compass, I'll roam far and wide,
Chasing whispers and wonders in a raucous ride.

The winds sing sweet melodies of silly delight,
In this raucous ballet, everything feels right.
With a wink from the stars, I'll sing with glee,
For in these wild whispers, I find the key.

So let the wildness tickle your soul,
In the heart of the chaos, we find our whole.
With smiles and the laughter that twinkles above,
We'll dance in the madness, with chaos, my love!

Greet the Unruly

With open arms, I greet what's tough,
For unruliness is often the best kind of stuff.
In mismatched shoes, I waddle along,
Singing a tune that feels all wrong.

The misfit parade marches down my street,
Parrots in bow ties? A dandy sweet treat!
With paint-splattered faces, we frolic and play,
In the friendly wildness, we'll brighten the day.

Tickle the fumble, embrace the peculiar,
For life's delicious chaos, let's all be a seer.
With giggles and snorts, we'll tumble anew,
Greet the unruly; it's where we all grew!

So come, lend your laughter, let's share the cheer,
In the symphony of madness, we have no fear.
Together, we'll marvel at life's silly twirl,
In the dance of the bizarre, let's give it a whirl!

Within the Maelstrom's Heart

In the maelstrom of life, I find my delight,
With whirlwinds of joy that twirl through the night.
My compass is silly; my map is a grin,
Navigating chaos is where to begin.

With kites made of cupcakes, I float with the breeze,
While doggies in sunglasses dash through the trees.
Rainbows painted boldly, in brilliant arrays,
Dash through the muddle with wild, wacky ways.

Bouncing with laughter, I tumble and spin,
Through the chaos of life, I revel within.
For each swirl of the storm brings treasures to find,
In the heart of the maelstrom, good fortune entwined.

So let wobbly whispers and giggles abound,
As I dance through the madness, where joy can be found.
With a twinkle of mischief, I choose to depart,
Living boldly and freely, within chaos's heart!

www.ingramcontent.com/pod-product-compliance
Lightning Source LLC
Chambersburg PA
CBHW072215070526
44585CB00015B/1354